LULLABY
FOR SINNERS

ALSO BY KATE BRAVERMAN

Lithium for Medea (a novel)
Milk Run

LULLABY
FOR SINNERS

Poems

Kate Braverman

HARPER & ROW, PUBLISHERS, New York
Cambridge, Hagerstown, Philadelphia, San Francisco,
London, Mexico City, São Paulo, Sydney

1817

I wish to express my gratitude to Leland Hickman
for his help with this book.

K.B.

Grateful acknowledgment is made for permission to reprint:

"Clockman," "Cobalt Blue," "Two and One-Half Years Ago," "This Is a Rented City," "Soon," "Details," "What Men and Women Do," "Posing," "My Husband Who Is Not" (My Husband Who Is Not My Husband), "Lies," "When the Dogs Bark," "7 P.M.," "April in Paris," and "Milk Run," all of which originally appeared in *Milk Run* by Kate Ellen Braverman. Copyright © Kate Ellen Braverman 1977. Reprinted by permission.

"Meeting the Palm Reader," "Fall Rain, Fall Wind and Leaf," and "Plague Suite" originally appeared in *Bachy 13*.

"West Indies Song" ("West Indies Prayer") originally appeared in *Bachy 16*.

"Faircrest Avenue," "Last of the Line," "By Madness Wooed," and "For My Unborn Daughter" originally appeared in *NEW*.

"Rushing" originally appeared in *Little Caesar 8*.

"Birthplace" and "Lullaby for Sinners" originally appeared in *Contemporary Quarterly*.

"Angeles Crest Highway" originally appeared in *Choice*.

"You Sigh Arctic White" originally appeared in *The Dream Journal*.

"One Month, Perhaps Two" originally appeared in *Foreign Exchange*.

"Spell" originally appeared in the *L.A. Weekly*.

FIRST EDITION

Designed by Lydia Link

Library of Congress Cataloging in Publication Data

Braverman, Kate.
  Lullaby for sinners.
  I. Title.
PS3552.R3555L8   811'.54   79-2729
ISBN 0-06-010439-2

80 81 82 83 84 10 9 8 7 6 5 4 3 2 1

For my mother, Millicent

Contents

CLOCKMAN

I have a certain appreciation
for precision and grace.
I never really liked this face.
An amputation, a graft,
a new combination
functional in all climates.

A known geometry.
You sit behind me.

It is by chance that I am here,
attracted by your neon sign.

    Old slides. Card Tricks. Dice.
    Monograms made to order—
    Your own initials if preferred.
    Time Travel Permits.
    Vitamin E.
    Forged Documents.

Complete personality kits.
Shall I assemble mine now?
You will have to write in Braille.
I am verbal but limited
by events beyond concise detail.

One torn paper parasol lying on a lawn.
Quiet streets. Afternoon.
An old woman sweeping a porch.
I seem to have lost my gloves.
There was a storm this morning.
I knitted my son a sweater.
Once I watched a spaceship land.
I keep a collection of rare, fine fevers.

I know perfectly well what you mean,
do you want me to scream?

Clockman,
cutting on the dotted line.
See, I brought mine.
Under the dress, across the flesh.
I can meet you in the parking lot.
A country setting could be arranged.
Here are scars from the last incision.
I never killed a baby.
You've confused me
with some other lady.
And now,
about the prescription?

Sunlight striking cement
still seems more delicate
than snow.
The sky is uneventful,
my fists healing well.
When the bandages are removed,
symmetry improved
then will I have to leave?

Clockman,
you sit behind me.
Cartographer, director of expeditions.
I have kept nothing hidden.
Witness this exorcism exhibition.
I, a one-woman show.
Monday, Wednesday, Friday
one-fifteen to two.

COBALT BLUE

The winter I learned colors
my father got the cobalt blues.
He bled in his sleep
the week we learned apple red.
Friday is white and black
throwing stones in the snow
by the railroad tracks.
The neighbor boy
vying for the gold star whispers
your father's dying.

He drinks milkshakes after treatments,
spends entire days in bed.
She brings him lunch on a tray.
I collect clay models, fossils,
the transformation of a butterfly.
But this big man is becoming a boy.

We move next door with neighbors.
Raking leaves, cutting knees,
pushing rag dolls in backyard swings.
Driving to town for matinees,
monster movies, mutants in the woods,
atomic wars.
Worlds where all things were scarred,
like a knife criss-crossing
someone's father's throat.

Preparing for the inevitable,
she cancels my piano recital.
A stream of strangers
wander our corridors
buying brass lamps,
the new china plates.
A truck waits.
Men load crates.
Leaves fall outside a screen door.
She touches his flesh.
The winter I learned colors
she was twenty-six.

TWO AND ONE-HALF YEARS AGO

Two and one-half years ago
the walls had begun pulsating.
There were gaps everywhere.
Faces would gather momentum
and disintegrate like organic
building blocks falling down.
    Floating down, really.

I ate breakfast at sunset,
drinking wine and sleeping pills,
laughing and crashing into doors,
setting sofas on fire.

I went to buy cigarettes
at the Shell Service Station
at Third and Robertson.
A man walking a dog
found me.
I was admitted as an O. D.

The long lines of fluorescent lights
looked sticky, like rotten marshmallows.
The sky was a basket of ruined fruit.
They made me vomit the burgundy,
the Tuinal, Seconal, Valium.
They made me vomit
popsicles eaten at seven,
peaches from summer camp,
slices of wedding cake.

They wanted to know about goals.
I've never been careful,
I told them.
I miss so much as it is.
If I were careful, God,
I would miss it all.

THIS IS A RENTED CITY

This is a rented city.
Born fully formed.
A monopoly board with orange trees.
The desert coughs under the weight
of trucked-in tons of concrete.

Bungalows squat on square lawns
pitted by rainbirds.
Sun squeezes through venetian blinds,
filling floors with shadowy knives.

There is danger
too distant to be a factor.
Earthquakes last only seconds.
It is too much to hope for.

There is a slow rotting.

A dog or a fern is worth
more than a woman.
They have clinics for killing babies.
There are mutants at the laundromat,
driving buses and making change.
Decipher the hum in elevators:

    It is warm here.
    You don't need a job here.
    I will grow peaches and avocados for you.
    Man, you don't even need shoes.

The pioneer stock is stopped
by the sheer blue cliffs of the sea.
They wander with packs on their backs,
praying for destruction by comet
and worshipping the Joshua tree.
They are ancient at eighteen,
veterans of nirvana and hell.

The future is flat,
etched in stucco
where there are no war lords,
merely slum lords,
the brown haze, the dead wind.
But no ovens, no conflagrations.
Not even the humanity
of the gas chambers.

SOON

I will be still soon.
I am ready as burnt red leaves,
edges arched like claws at the sky.
I will drift and fall
where there are no parking tickets,
divorces, infidelity or lies.
No fainting in public places
waking to nurses in pink sweaters
with wheelchairs and ammonia.

I want the dirt weight.
Land masses slide together.
The ice sheets shift.
New maps are printed.
But the cycle is old
and certain of itself.
The fine brown hand
of the earth covers.
There is no coughing,
no visions of birds,
aluminum or parking structures.
The bones are pure
and last forever.
In time lost pieces are reunited.
Secretions from sheets,
then triangular nails bitten
and flicked across a rug.
The hair grows luxuriant.
It takes centuries
for the body to be complete.

Then I will soften
cell by cell.
Without double yellow lines,
checkbooks or felonies.
I will know the dirt.
It will be my right to refuse
roots and rebirths.
I will be a large forgetful worm.
I will burrow and be still.

DETAILS

I must remember the details.
Sunlight on the blond hairs
of your arm.
Moods changing your eyes
now gray, now blue.

Already it begins.
The blank stormy slide
into that other side.

When you know the chairs
and have worn a path
through the carpets
you will dust me off
like a prop,
tell me when to dance,
when to lie still
and shut up.

Before I must start flirting
with pills and the car exhaust
in my hunger for the dark,
the black arms you will awaken.

Already they are scratching.
The walking death.
I am inhabited.
Small things, dwarves
or lost children
sing in my garden.
I cannot see them.
They skirt past my eyes,
a patch of fast black.
It always begins this way.

I must remember your fingers
breaking French bread,
brushing the crumbs
on your pants leg.
Your profile while you cut cheese.
The knife in your hand
and your smile.

WHAT MEN AND WOMEN DO

Even behind shades
neon twists limbs to stalks.
These are not arms and legs
but leafy branches.
And those must be roots
rustling across your thigh,
arching to my mouth
a small sun.
Belly to belly
there is no air.

It is strange
what men and women do.

You lean on one elbow
lighting a cigarette
telling me of a girl
twelve years ago,
parked near bushes
feeding on your fibers
making maps with her tongue.
In the darkness
where there are no faces,
no voices
only wind playing with branches
I offer to kiss her
sixteen-year-old mouth with you.
In half-light
you are thick and sharp as a knife.
Your face swollen
pale and enormous
heavier than darkness
mouth half-open
moaning my name.

It is strange
what men and women do.

The body is made whole
by sunlight.
The mirror confirms
the expected arrangement.
You select clothing from a closet
and brush leaves from your flesh.
A man again,
strapping time to your wrist.

POSING

The wood is ripped in a thin patch.
My brother fell in a tight angry
bundle against it,
aiming for your chest
the day before we went to Spain.
The stairs are still lined
with cardboard cartons,
a series of strange tan ornaments.
The draft. Pinto beans simmering.
The plants on the landing.
The mirror you found.

We sit in the kitchen.
The day drifts out to sea.
The sun hangs at the edge,
is punctured, spilling
one fine plum and coral line.
Lamplight rustles the leaves
and takes the curtains
like a pale pair of wings.
You pour beans into a bowl.
The buildings on the boulevard
huddle together,
rows of stone children
called into supper.
Glued down with gray paste
for the night.

You mix pinks and peach
on your glass palette
I assume my pose.
I have been practicing all week,
not scratching or coughing
barely breathing.
I am stiller than your lemons
on kitchen counters,

your rotting piers
with dark, stranded legs
and antique tables with
thrift store lamps.

Perhaps you will give me
shoulders today.
I could use them
and arms.
And thick strips of white
for the torn places,
residues from accidents.
If you ask, I will say
I was not born
but assembled by blind men
from scraps.

MY HUSBAND WHO IS NOT MY HUSBAND

My husband who is not my husband
sleeps face up,
a pale beached sea mammal
dragging air through an opening
snoring, farting with impunity.
Naked, in sunlight and old slippers
he is sniffing in my kitchen.
He will have eggs sunnyside up,
toast and peppermint tea.
(But he will not marry me.)
He is afraid his paintings won't sell.
Or that I and the small
chromosome-damaged bawling morons
will grow fat from his art.
He thinks it better now
with us lean,
and the hallway so empty
you can hear old pins breathe.
He calls me girlfriend,
though I am old and plump
as a wife
and faithful.
He is uncertain.
I drink too much.
He wants me to smile more.
He says I whisper in corners
with my mother.
He is too clever.
(This is not the first time.)
My husband who is not my husband
will not even speculate
on the colors and shapes
of babies unborn,
curled on the dusty shelves
of my belly.

LIES

You say I lay for years
in the fleshy web of your shoulder
feeding on your hot salty milk
moaning, twisted in sheet
our hips twin hills.
Lies.
Your bed is pure and unscarred,
thick walls shutting out
Washington Boulevard.
Your skin is clear of indentations.
You are untouched,
first generation Los Angeles
with even white teeth.
Your legacy of balanced meals
and music lessons after school.
Your fat mother in her kitchen
punctual, begging you for one
more spoon of vegetables.
Fearing your withdrawal,
temper and scorn.
You, the first born son.
Living six years above a bar.
Tending your collections
of tropical fish, pennies
in jars, parts of bicycles.
Inching into madness
in silence, by degree.
Savoring the experience.
The things that simply happen
when you can refuse nothing.
The strange women disrobing
leaving behind pieces of themselves.
A chair upholstered in velvet,
a satin vest, pressed flowers
in a coffee cup.

You say I laughed
and made gardens of window ledges.
Lies.
The window sills are empty.
The street is dulled by fog.
You, sleep well.

WHEN THE DOGS BARK

When the dogs bark
from a fenced yard
on Washington Boulevard
I think you are coming
with black face and ax,
fangs bared.

This sheet is thin.
It cannot protect me.
Your ears are pointed now.
I must still my dull heart beating
in this dull August heat.
It is a drum to you.

Men are like dogs.
Pet them.
They will crawl into your lap.
But never let them smell the fear,
hot and intoxicating.
They can snap limbs.
You cannot sing to them.
They will bury your bones
in an alley
for a rainy day.

Feed them.
They will stay with you.
Bellies bloated, eyes red
listless in a thick sleep.
But in their dreams
they are stalking dark streets,
pissing on lampposts
howls ripping their throats:

Oh moon, moon
too cold and far away
to fuck.

7 P. M

It's the quality of the light
that excites me.
The small safe arcs
in a herd of restless dark things
feeding on the soft edges
of the room,
in black puddles of tar
where strangers lose their bones.

It's a 7 P. M. in Hollywood yellow.
Whore yellow. Junky yellow.
A world of old dressing tables
stained with divorce and migraines.

A bad hour for decisions.
Shadows prepare an invasion
while I run the bath.
The truth is swollen shut.
I cannot touch it,
even with my tongue.
I will always marry the wrong men.
None of them will do.
Not with surgery and therapy,
protein and new clothing.
Not tonight or next year or ever.

There are no answers in the mirror,
smoking dope, putting on make-up,
pretending I'm a jazz singer
in a backstage dressing room.

This is the hour the men return
empty and dry as old milk bottles.

APRIL IN PARIS

Mother, forgive my silence
in Paris
in our Hotel on Rue Scribe
where the salon was always empty
and the chandelier was thinning
like tinsel on a Christmas tree
in March.

Ten days of my temper and moods,
refusing everything
from Boulevard de Capucines
to the flea market at Clignancourt.
An insomniac who couldn't wake up,
intimidated by the City of Light
and your appetite.

You ground my shoes down to nails.
I coughed and couldn't keep up.
The river was not enough.
You wanted more. Bridges,
monuments, both banks.
You could have walked to Normandy
in your fur coat and tennis shoes,
your seven weeks of Berlitz.

Couldn't you see the river
contained no water,
simply stale things
hopeless and gray?
I felt my toes turning to stones.
I would never return.
I would become the spine
of a sixteenth-century bridge,
catatonic and without eyes.
We lunched on a boat
but I could not eat.
Even my breath seemed old.

In the Tuileries
you touched pink and red
flowers to your lips.
You wanted to name
and breathe everything,
the alleys of the Latin Quarter,
each rung on the Eiffel Tower.
You circled the tomb at Les Invalides,
a panther asking exact dimensions,
settling questions of granite
or agate.

I stood mute and haunted
while you argued with tour guides
demanding the perfect seats,
the high ones
where the view was complete.
I could not look at your eyes
huge and brown, flecked with gold,
New York's slum child made good
in a city of light gray and rose.

This is your hour.
It has taken forty-five years,
a small matter.
Now the banners are hung
and the fountains carved
for you alone to devour.

MILK RUN

I was the rag doll
you wanted in childhood,
on the stoops of other people's
houses and lives.
You even ironed the ribbons
on my baby smocks.

So what if I coughed
and was born scratching my eyes
and needed special silk mittens
to guard against damage?

You were a brunette,
chain smoking and baking pies.
You woke me at 3 a. m.
to drink hot chocolate
in the cold old kitchen
and watch the first snow fall.
Rain.
A lonely wet robin
built a nest in a low branch.
We watched him struggle.

Mother, your hair has turned
yellow.
Everything is yellow.
California.
The sun falls into the ocean.
I am ten and puffy
in second-hand party dresses,
failing math, needing eyeglasses
friendless and waiting for you.

But your bedroom door is closed
while you cry over conspiracies.
The foster homes
where they gave you scraps
from their plates
and you never had a key,
not even in winter.

Then the gambler husband
who got cancer.
Now this daughter.
Pale, afraid of everything
the strange slatted trees
the thick sunlight.
A girl with nightmares
and bad posture
no one will want.

Mother, why do you come home
so late?
I grow hair under my arms
but you don't notice.
You are dressed for work,
black high heels and floppy hat.
I could never be as pretty as you,
even when you cry,
hurling yourself against my locked door,
shouting while the wood breaks
and beating my face
with your hairbrush.
And you never ask about boys.

Then the fat one comes
to marry me.
We are both saved.
What does it matter
if his parts don't work,
if his thing coils in his lap
like a plump dead worm?
I got the ring.
I go to college, collect recipes.
What does it matter
if my hands shake
and I take sleeping pills?
I can be patched, mended.
At nineteen
nothing is permanent.
Not even the fat boy,

who can't talk anymore
and mumbles and sleeps
on the floor.
He'll become a professor
if he survives.

Mother, what color is your hair?
We live on different sides
of the city,
a flat no man's land between us.

You did not know the second one.
He had a sick smell
of dark rooms and smoke
enameled to his skin.
Past marriages clung
to his pale flesh
like nets with sharp edges.
Silence drew his lips
tight and frozen
like fish strangled on hooks
or impaled roses.

Now my lovers fix
the things that break,
fasten lightbulbs and hang shelves.
They take nothing.
There is nothing left to take.

In the early mornings
palm trees sway
in a light that is perfect,
thin, exquisite
covering the gutters
of Washington Boulevard
in the softest gauze.
My fingers are naked.
By choice I sleep alone.
Mother, from here on
it's a milk run.

BIRTHPLACE

What is this
that picks and scratches
at the edges?
You return to it
as you must.
It is your birthplace,
the stars that pin you
with the glorious eyes
of frenzied prophets.
Why bend bitterly
at hollows
where nothing grows
but darkness
and the outline
of an empty hand?
The revelation is the branch
and the slice of shadow.
You will collapse naked
and wordless
as you were at the beginning,
blinded by morning
gasping and cursed.
See the cycles etched
even in the cool paths
near your soul.
Your throat is filled
with round stones.
The discs of moon
grow fat and scatter
in seasons measured
only by grain in rock.
The moment breaks.
It cannot bask like a slow
dull animal in the sun
forever.
Open your hands, goddamn it.
Move.

FIRST LOVE

I knew I could grow things.
Barelegged without panties or shoes.
My breasts were warm ridges
suddenly glued to my chest.
The unnamed place between my legs
was a dark nest filled with red eggs.
I was careful where I sat.

The city opened.
Not boulevards with billboards
but yes, a garden.
I rode buses at random
to the peeling buildings
bordering vacant lots
where old men sat with bottles
on broken doorsteps.
My feet were calloused
from streets of softening tar,
invisible vines.
Mother called me wild.

My Irish boyfriend from Georgia
was eighteen with a crucifix
above his bed, a pawnship ruby ring
and a blood-red Chevrolet.
He bit my breasts
and gave me cigarettes.
We stole hubcaps in alleys
and threw them into the sea.
We broke and entered an abandoned motel
and made love on a gutted cot
on top of blood stains
while rain fell.

I did not know I was wounded then.
I only remember his legs
with long black curling hairs
that seemed to be reaching for me

and the ruby ring on the nightstand.
There are no names for these things.
They do not wash away or erode.
They are dark thorns in the flesh.
Lie if you must.
Call it what it never was.
First love.

FAIRCREST AVENUE

I return by bus
even when I walk
or drive my car.
It is the drained blue
of the blue buses
of my youth.
The Western Line
with the blue veins
of Pico, Olympic, Santa Monica.
    The world neatly contained
    between three boulevards
winding down at the thin breakwater
and one gull beyond the washed rock.

I stop at Pico Boulevard
my anchor, unchanging.
    Herbie's Fine Meats,
    the laundry, bakery and camera shop.
The seasons of Pico Boulevard
are white hot or stinging gray
at Christmas,
    with lights strung on poles,
    glitter in the palms,
    the shop windows brushed
    with machine frost.
Dusk is a cold splinter
as I walk from the school bus
with the books I never read.
The deformed sun dissolves
at my back
    spitting sick orange blood
    on the pavement, the poinsettias,
    the cats just fed and exiled
    to side streets with trimmed bushes.

Up, wind brushed, up
a small hill,
a hump struggling from the curb

covered with thinning ivy
    planted by my father
    turning brown always, and dying.
The rounded sides of orange tiles
form a low domed roof on the garage
jammed with old newspapers
still with red rubber bands
across their throats
    tossed by little boys
    on bicycles
    who know better than to stop.

I follow the narrow gorge
of steep cement carved
between house and ivy
to the sliding-glass back door.
    There is my father
    installed in a corner,
    a dark appliance, faulty,
    with wiring rotting,
    sending strange charges.
Hello, Daddy.
    Fermenting near the wall,
    altering your molecular structure.
Hello, Daddy.
    Inching into the black zone,
    as the sun goes down, still
    able to shake it off with morning.

My father brings his corner
with him.
It could be the cool center
of the room.
He sucks in all the air
    giving birth to vacuums,
    cursing, the veins in his neck
    throbbing, his fist balled up tight
    and breaking a window.

Daddy is calling me to supper,
laughing, spooning rich meats
on my plate.
More than I could ever eat
but do.
Daddy is staring at me
his face cluttered
    yelling You're too fat,
    too fat. He grabs my plate
    making it shatter at my feet
    making me shield my face.
He leaves me with splinters
while he watches golf
and falls asleep on the couch.

Is that my mother?
    High heels on sunbaked cement,
    arms wrapped around folders
    and homework.
She pulls apart the glass doors,
sinks into the closest chair
exhausted, pouring Scotch.
She eats scrambled eggs alone.
He is sleeping.
We are afraid to talk.
    I hear her running a hot bath.
    Wrestling becomes bowling.
She pulls the covers over
her head.

What is this shrieking,
this breaking?
Hello, Mother,
screaming, packing a suitcase
at midnight,
    a pale shape by lamplight,
    crying as the wind blows
    her tight scarf to one side.

She crumples on the stubby wet
grass in front of the house
    as a lone car passes near her head,
    a porch light next door flicks on
    while spit forms a fine line
    along her lip.
My father brings her back.

Here is the house at dusk.
Innocuous, the shame covered
with fresh pastel paint.
Here is the hate.
And here is the bamboo gate
in the piece of fenced patio
where my father sits
    silent and impossible
    as the banana plants
    along the hedge.
Here is the path down
to Faircrest Avenue.
Faircrest.
What did it sound like to her?
    Collecting the down payment.
    Promising them anything
    after the Bronx childhood
    of cold stoops and red bricks.
    After the hospitals.
Faircrest.
    The curling of clear blue
    mountain air in a kingdom
    nestled between Pico and Olympic
    where the past overlaps.
And him? The master at last
    with built-in barbecue,
    rainbirds, leaves to sweep.
A man of property
in a land of second chances.

There is the retired rabbi
in the pink house
on the other side of the street,
on its own lump of green.
He never spoke to us
     even when he walked his dog
     past the place where my father
     stood watering his balding ivy.
They said we fought
and made the dogs bark.
Twice they called police.
And no one said good-by
when strangers came on Sundays
and they saw the Sold sign
stuck by the curb.

But I am back,
back with a bus.
And everyone is coming.
     My father. The newspaper boys.
     My mother. The rabbi with his dog.
     Yes, the dog is coming.
The bus is taking everything.
     The Christmas lights.
     The summers.
     The goddamn ivy.
It's all of Faircrest Avenue
in the blue bus of my youth.
And finally I am driving,
taking them all down Pico Boulevard
and not stopping.
     Do you understand?
     Not for popcorn or the highway.
     Scream your throat raw.
This bus is going out to sea.

THE LAST OF THE LINE

The women are leaving slowly
hobbling on broken feet.
Let me tell you
of the binding of feet in China,
the custom for a millennium.
At age three
the soft flesh was sealed
in special sheets.
How they stank in summer.
A necessary preparation
for the woman stink.
The summers were torn
by girl children
screaming in their sleep
as the bones crushed in.
The ideal was two inches.
The toes fell off, of course.
The mother, stumbling
on her crippled lumps,
cautioned at the crib.
Be thankful the earth
coughed crops that year,
or you would have been
drowned.
Girl child, with the nest
that bleeds and grows things.
She must be tamed,
carried on a litter
like a trophy that breathes.
You cannot trust her.
The forests are full of madwomen
living in caves, eating
grasshoppers and howling.

They did not speak
of drowning me,
though it was a poor year
and snowing.

Slowly, I entered the world
of the girl child.
I was polished silver and silk.
I was Christmas lists
and shopping lists
and lists of names for babies.
Remember Aunt Ruth, Mother whispers,
forty, a drunk,
with eyeglasses and no child,
the last of the line.
Everyday hoping,
with my shoes shined
and my armpits smelling
of flowers,
of lilacs and jasmines
(the oils that run the world).
Perhaps tomorrow.
The one who anoints
with a snap of his fingers
and takes the sting
out of darkness.

Of course, you know these things.
How it is in the parking lot,
gliding into your slot,
pushing your cart down the aisles,
packing and unpacking
and picking up crumbs.
(There it is again.)
Looking too often at the leg.
A feeling of invisibility.
The ache, the scream
as it pushes out.
Then you know
there are two of you.
You become fat
or take a lover,
but it keeps shoving,

a pale new you within.
One day you limp
to the window
and find the roads filled
with refugees.
It surprises, at first.
The sheer number of women
hobbling, selling everything.
The linen hooks, the porcelain hooks.
They have been in the quarry
and scraped the mountain clean.

SPELL

It rained the rain of curses
and world's end.
Puddles erupted in the plaza
outside the cathedral in Palma
in an unnaturally windy October
two months before you left me

at Christmas, in Los Angeles
my hands frozen on tinsel,
breathless and stunned
gasping for air.
I was one entire year drunk
with grief.

May you have a nest of squalling
infants, stupid women, plants
that die, illness and the endless
redress of sunset.

Once I loved you softly
lazy as a wife hanging sheets
in noon sun,
accepting the parallel lines
of our life,
that impossible balancing act.

May your autumn be indecently callous,
prolonged and broken.
May winter strike without warning,
a series of sponged thin afternoons
withering and spilling their guts
on your lawn.

May you be empty and cut
and know the moon is a monster
and night poisonous,
black as a sea of rats.

May you sleep with fever
and splintered dreams
and sense me, incandescent
with the unspeakable malice
I will you in this life
and all others.

FIRST NIGHT

I

Slow pulse of morning, snakeskin
of sheet, the tumbling into the thin
ripening crevice of noon

and a lover packed off to Boston cobble-
stones, the River Charles I've never seen
but imagine as echoing footsteps

across a bridge in star-sheen
like Strawberry Creek in Berkeley
in winter, stones at Sather Gate

and further, beneath the campanile
granite lions frozen, eyes carved
open and tortured by moon.

II

When my brother Hank was a child
he loosened his mouth into an O
and hopped at the full moon, angry

in his prototype conflict with women,
their cold brutal power
and radium flowers.

Once he cut up my rag doll
seaching for doll-bones, doll-blood,
a sliver of beating pin-cushion heart.

The emptiness startled him, lifeless
feathers, his assumptions in question.
The first girl-body a shell of lies.

III

Thickening day, middle-aged, matronly
hips like a field in a fat breeze.
Don't struggle with that summer frock.

Garish fool, the best has been.
The man is gone, walks cobblestones
after a first night, his body alien

as another species, humanoid perhaps,
with scales and claws, his odd residue
a white stab of moonlight, quartz eggs,

granite discs and stone O's inside me.
A hard alphabet, birthless, persistent.
Nothing grows. His name was Phillip.

MY GARDEN

All day there is the press
of you, you accusing
from the dusty corners,
the edge of the unmade bed.

I spend days in my tiny garden,
an anomaly stuck and forgotten
between factory buildings.
I watch fall take your ferns.
Only my nightshade and hemlock
grow invisibly, a searing green
burning my eyelids.

You will find me in wind
complaining, hallucinating,
wanting too much
when I should be baking
and singing haunting lullabies
while watching the clock
and soaping and douching
and polishing my cunt.
My how time flies.

Listen.
I have been skinned
in slow motion, beginning
with the fleshy pads
of my palms,
that hidden nest of taut nerves
punctured with wide black holes.
I am dark and shy,
manic, impossible.

I did not expect necrophiliacs
this soon.
My flesh is loose, white,
an insect's feast.
Bill collectors. Police.

My father sixty-two now
without grandchild.

Fall rattles the garden wall.
Violated trees gasp for breath.
I am always half-asleep.
Ice hangs on my leg bones.
Laughter cuts sudden channels
in my throat.
I cough, smoke tumbles my lips.

You'd do well not to come
back at all.

ONE MONTH, PERHAPS TWO

One month, perhaps two.
I'm just finishing up.
Mopping a bit,
locking the shop.
The gate on severed hinges
can keep kicking the dirt
like a hanged man.
Let the strongest weeds
prevail.

It will do for now.
I won't be around next fall.
No license renewals
or Christmas rush.
I don't can my fruit now.
I eat it until I'm sick
or step on it,
the oranges and peaches.
I watch them rot.

It's not elegant anymore.
Retching at midnight.
Cold water hasn't helped
in weeks.
Poisonous things run loose
in me, leaping wild
between cells,
sending scrambled messages.
Do I hear voices?

Could I show you something
in a church choir?
You want it smaller?
I've got little boys and dogs.
Shrieks. A rape track
you can play in your car,
amuse your friends,
impress the boss.
What?

You like my pots?
Gifts from a first marriage
stained by two dozen sinks.
They still stink of him.
How about the chipped plates
in conflicting patterns,
the half-made curtains
and broken lamps?
I'll get you a shopping bag.

One month, perhaps two.
I'll never read Lorca
in Spanish, or dance,
even once, in silk
to my ankles.
I'm short on regrets.
I'll take fire or worms.
Or strap me to a raft.
Let me drift purple
in the sea-swell,
inexhaustible, yes.

JOURNEY/PRAYER

I

Your grandfather beckons
with carved stone fingers.
Heed.
Never leave this parched valley.
Live as he lived.

Pick the red fruit with thorns.
Feed them to pigs sliding
on their dirt-matted sides,
crushing their young.

Poke the earth with sticks
while clouds crash together
and their offspring is wheat
is maize and oats.
Crop high; and half-hidden
calloused harvest hands clap
with the jubilation of idiots.

Can't you see the old man's eyes
are chiseled and empty?
He has stood half asleep
for centuries.
His measurements are false
are lies
are the piece of a broken vase
dug up by strangers.

Do you think you are blessed
in the granite calendars
tracing the paths of stars
and your grandfather's comet
coming again and again?
This is the flight of birds only.

II

Beyond the backyard
lies the whole world.

You could sweep the pieces
to the ground,
walk to the post office
and never return.

There is no license for this,
no dress rehearsal.
Asphalt would become dirt.
Wire fences would dissolve.
No one will follow.

III

Embrace the night.
Try to shake from it
one simple yes or no.
Your arms with cut tunnels
in blackness.
It will take your breath
and pronounce you small.
The night is hollow.
It laughs and rattles
and breaks apart.
It will never answer.

Search the moon for solace.
She will remain silent,
an accidental beacon, a cyst,
dead to your curses
or cursed herself,
a mere witness.

There is not strength
or faith enough for this.
Your eyes will be dried
and bleached.
Your hands will tremble
and fill with scars.
But it's yours,
absolutely yours.

FOR MY UNBORN DAUGHTER

You nestled with me in February.
I sat at an upstairs desk
planning your black hair,
your small breasts.
I will tell you secrets,
my flesh, my air.
You were with me before the one
who calls himself father.
He is the accident.
You were with me in the cold
dusk, house absolutely still.
I saw you in the mirror.
Rachel. Elizabeth. Heather. Grace.
I give you the names of bells
and snow.

This winter I have touched
the white acres of my childhood
freshly plowed to the graves
of your great-great grandmother
Katrina, that learned Polish witch
whose name I bear like a black truth.
And her insane red-haired daughter
Rose of the secrets, the sweat shops
and desertions.
Our line was born in farm lofts
and welfare hospitals sitting
in the torn intestines of poor cities
with the Cossacks coming,
the Nazis.
We were of the small dark rooms
where fear and pneumonia grew
between the candles, bony
blessed chickens and holy books.

You, my daughter, will take
your pleasures and griefs
at open windows with bougainvillea

in this white-hot southern city.
Perhaps your time will invent
again the alchemy in dirt-roots.
Land swells your skin.
I tell you, fruit will burst.
You have the calm strength of firs.
The tossed bones brought you here,
tarot cards and sirens.
You are the moment forced into form,
obdurate as shtetl stones.

MEETING THE PALM READER

Your hands are calloused.
You have abused your intellect
in the acquisition of archaic
phrases and books by the truck-
load, heavy as bricks.
There will come a reckoning.
Geometry will fail you.
You will be as an unsealed tomb
after generations naked to moon,
siltdrift and the frenzy
of small things hopping in ruin.
You will outwit nothing.
You will be as driftwood,
roots snapped, seacord cut.
Even the air will confuse.
Promises will be broken.
You will be alone,
without husband or children
and the core will remain hidden.
The canals you tread will dry
to listless mud and push
from their sides the objects
of your past.
Later, you will journey south
beneath storm clouds.
Obscure languages will taunt
and the jungle of damp
hibiscus and red flamboya
swallow you.
Dawn will be white
sun lost behind fog.
The borders will be erased.
You will enter the fast waters
and I tell you absolutely,
the sails will snap.

SHE

I rage and red
autumnal and partial
as an X ray,
a dream-thing and evil.
I sing on rocks
make ships crash.

This is my season
and inheritance,
the red charred leaf
the broken and unformed.
I am the plague
that will always come,
the intelligence swelling
rivers and tearing crops down.

I am blood.
I am infrared still-shot
of girl plucking apple,
the swallowed thorns,
the sin opening up each month
like a deranged clock.

I frightened even Father
when I stumbled from the rib
cradle all wrong
and he abandoned me
to the cobra
where I learned my name
witch/sphinx/bitch
and knew the stone altar
and stake.

I became what waits
for the hunter,
the trap and the web,
what remains
after the absolute sacrifice,

after the clean bone proof
and ash.
I am rage most exquisite
and blessed.
I am the dragon
on the final map.

RUSHING

Wild moths beat your eyes wide.
You are the candle and arc of light.
You find the fragile blue pulse.
You say it's all in the smell
of alcohol and ripening lemons.
The lightbulb, glistening yellow metal
like a captured moon might be.
It's sailing the harbor at Puerto Vallerta,
swimming warm water and black sharks
to a cove of wild boars and waterfalls
choked by ferns. You taste it,
filling your mouth and lungs
as you ride into the Salinas Valley
drought-hot November, vineyards
and walnut trees gone red.
It's behind your eyes.
It's on your tongue.
It's the field where Daddy took off
your training wheels and you careened
that first bicycle through stakes
of stiff ash-colored birch.
It's learning to tell time again
and not get in cars with strangers.
Thirteen years of psychiatry
and they're right. It's mother,
unbuttoning her blouse, giving you
her great white breast at last.
You bite through her startled
ribcage. It's day breaking over
Hollister, California, land of pine
cones and artichokes and hills
of horses caught behind the spoils
of fences as you ride to the white
caps and ice plant clawing the slow
dunes at Moss Landing, fields viridian,
fields salamander and coral, all edging
into harvest. And it's Mazatlán
and Moss Landing, Massachusetts

and Mallorca. My God, it's the fields
of Mars. Stiff winds cutting paths
through red grasses, beneath the twin
amber breasts before the moons
went blind and the vines dried.
So, you've swallowed it all.
Dust trails and dark ridge of shadow
gouged by a stagecoach ninety
years ago. Your arms?
Your arms have been carved by stars.
A Santa Ana wind slams through
your lungs. This is love, baby.
You are young, naked, your navel
filled with platinum. It's a sea
breeze curling in soft swirls
across cliffs just born on the moon.
And it's all of your childhood,
all at once, before you pull
the needle out.

YOU SIGH ARCTIC WHITE

You sigh arctic white.
The sea opens her icy lip.
Your path edges avalanches
and albino seals.
You are white under an empty
skull of sky.
Occasional powdery south-moving
clouds are fat with frozen bits
of your grandmother's bone,
an airborne virus of age.
You had to thread her needle.
Her knees were white islands.
She hemmed cotton curtains
filmy as her cataracts.
She sliced turkey on white linen.
Mistletoe and holly.
'Tis the season.
But you are white
in your own white season,
veins pumped full of white
narcotics drained from a moon.
And you have an entire family
at last, at Christmas.
You unwrap lace-up white
leather ice skates.
You are white beyond reason.

In the beginning white
amino acids strung
with white ribbons.
You are an infant amphibian
amazed by noon,
the white alphabet of bleached
sand and the litany of wind.
In the beginning chaos,
hunger and white gases,
ether and laughter.

Later, after starched lilies
and freshly painted fences,
after the ivory piano keys
and gouged aphrodisiac tusks
you wear the wedding dress,
the veil and perfect smile.
All winter you fill vases
with the most expensive
and frail white roses.
You know the true depths
of sea water as you drift
past the last reefs naked
in silk stockings.
Your lungs unfurl white
canvas across white caps
as you sail.

IMMOLATION

Six years in the underbelly of Los Angeles
baked white alleys, gash of wide gullies
where rain smaller than measurement licks
cement and dries without residue.
I will tell you what I know.

My garden trees struggle ambivalent.
Leaves never fall.
It's a matter of identity.
The white fingers, whittled winter branches
denied, denied.

That stolen birch is a lunatic.
Bougainvillea pushes insistent burgundy
crepe faces snaking up fences and roofs,
a useless bounty.
And paradise has failed me.

The hibiscus opens, a full cup of wine
or blood. My eyes dull to stiff canna,
the orange of lava, the sun enormous,
the iris pumping blooms, blooms
like poisoned tongues.

I have seen the sudden Santa Ana winds
sever the sagebrush and yucca.
Sleeping scorpions coiled under rock
and pried apart, bellies up to the moon,
those lethal cold rays.

My lovers burrow as night falls
in demonic black waves. We embrace
between hallucinations and shadows,
those nesting and dangerous dark bodies
glued like snails to the walls.

Afternoon is a white-out and seething.
Flesh wounds simmer and blister red,
red as the bleeding mouth of a rose.
The world shifts west into sunset,
that suicide serene at the immolation.

BY MADNESS WOOED

I was by madness wooed.
No flowers on porches with swings
and fireflies,
no wrapped-with-ribbon chocolates
but a stained brass lamp he found
sifting debris in a skid-row alley
on trash day.
He gave me a sun-smoothed stone
pried from a desert back road
when he was lost one high noon
just driving and collecting bits
of yucca gone gray and bony
as amputated fingers.
I loved this and his whispered
recitations of crimes and jails,
gay bars, police, whores, drugs.
His first wife a suicide.
He showed me scars where a knife
cut and the residues from accidents,
drunk nights and car crashes.
He grew orchids on his roof
and slept there in an August
of derelict hotels burning,
smoke rushing up like a gutted
down pillow into streets thick
and red with ambulances screaming
the air raw and bleeding.
He said he was wanted
by the State of Arizona
as if thousands of bodies
were waiting, writhing on sheets,
legs spread and begging
and I begged.

ANGELES CREST HIGHWAY

He says the women don't
matter, the ones he pays.
They're like the antique chairs
and thrift-store rugs he paints.
Still lifes. He tries not to touch.

The high desert coughs in your face.

He says the yucca in the snowbank
needs one special beetle to complete
its sexual cycle, that short season
when it pushes out a massive mid-section,
explodes the thighs and lays down

a suggestion of shell.

He drives the back roads from Los Angeles.
Riverside, Victorville and Crestline
hang on his belt like scalps.
Sand feeds him, cold splinters of sky.
You've never understood this man

or why you need him.

Surely another could have tied
your wrists with red velvet ribbons
and made your hidden parts open,
glistening, a collection of starsides,
a whirlpool, a phenomenon,

girl, girl, girl.

He says he's going to paint
a woman swinging naked next.
You think of her young legs floating
above a tapestry of rug as he drives
into an icy late-afternoon mist.

You sled into a creek of just-melted

snow and lay in the white and cold,
wet, afraid to breathe or move.
He's standing on the hilltop
above you, above the timberline
where trees twist bizarre and unkept

like the savages at the end of a race.

OASIS

April and impossible, this yawning mouth
of spring and hibiscus waving red fists
at a sun punched open above ripening lemons
and cutting flowers, poppies and carnations—

What is that sound? Who comes?
Why it's all the men I've ever loved
returning like the swallows.

I brush their hair and bathe them,
at peace with the birthdays they forgot
and the rare and obscenely ill-chosen gifts
in useless and tacky pink.
The beast is known now and tame.

My first husband waves, bleached and myopic,
his face pale in stinging spring air.
Comrade, I call, Brother.
Remember the revolution?
The Berkeley barricades?

And the Spanish bartender in Ibiza
who refused me five nights in a row,
my lips painted red and nipples sunburned
and hard in a skin-tight Paris sheath.
I drank myself sick and swam hopeless
in the long white noon, naked and moaning:
Carlos, Carlos, while the Mediterranean ran
into the wound, the sin silky and thick
by moonlight. He was married.

My dark Jewish lover appears after five
years of persistent desire, fade in/fade out
wisp and flutter of stabbed shut doors,
house of invisible clawed birds,
hemp-web of ingratitude and drugs.
The reconciliations of his slow black tongue.

Now, drunk on it, spinning and intoxicated
I see sun blessing and burning clean
beer stains in Ensenada motel rooms,
afternoons embedded like permanent wounds,
youth a blood-clot of savage unnecessary rage.
Noon of the pronged sharp teeth.

Come, my swallows, my white ones.
I will rock you in arms soft
as a new grave, arms long
as the roads we plunged across
the Southwest on.

Be still, my sweet broken ones.
Be gentle.

Take this unexpected oasis in April.
My darlings, sun dries blood.
My frail ones, salt air cures.
See, my garden is whole again,
bent under canna, walls of iris,
dazzle of red.

Even the earth forgives.

FALL RAIN, FALL WIND AND LEAF

Fall rain, fall wind and leaf.
Wash the parched emaciated flesh
and heaps of ash in the gutters.
Make new trout brooks and green.
Bring the mysterious illness west,
the chill, the fever swells
and necessary deaths.
Let them at the edge tumble
and bury their small miseries.

We bent too long to the summer,
that deranged widow howling
all August through the morphine,
cursing the nurses and daughter
who crossed the country to comb
the old woman's hair at midnight
and hold the discolored claw
of a hand, touching the erratic
pulse with her tongue knowing
forgiveness would be denied.

Fall rain, fall wind and leaf.
Bring the sudden cold
and abandonment, the loss
of trust, the rush of a shapeless
hungry black space drunk on itself.
Let us camp on the banks of fat
rivers and forget our thirst
and walking sores and the tangled
cities perched in the lap
of dying seas where we have
too long tended the graves
of those we love.

PLAGUE SUITE

In the ruin, plague carts pass.
The dead in sacks are consigned
to absolute sleep beneath streetlamps
and the shallow drained banks
of useless clouds poised
above the shell of the city,
above the dog packs on old walkways
littered with yellow and red
shreads of summer awnings.

Rumors of unnatural cold
persist.

The man and woman have grown
their own contagion in the dust
and dazed insects they sleep upon.
A rain of wind born tin cans
and severed vegetation scratches.
A billboard is slashed in two
by a black sea breeze.
Broken cathedral bells ring twelve,
continual twelve bleeding into twelve.
It is always midnight, the hour
of final betrayal.

In the plague zone, no doors
lock.

The man finds a stick
and sharpens it.
He could become a corner bandit,
find women hiding canned goods
under their skirts.
He wonders why dog teeth glisten
yellow and dreams he is sleeping
in the lap of rusty train tracks
under a gigantic lid of white moon.

The woman's arms pin him
like a stake.
He twists into the nest of dark
vague with fever and longing
and makes a list of all the ways men
can die and recites it,
alphabetically, a kind of litany:
O arrows, O bullets, O cholera,
demons, entropy, gas.

Dawn is stripped and smoky.
The man and woman shiver
in the guts of a cellar,
coughing up pieces of lung
like green marbles.

They watch the city burn.

THESE THINGS HAPPEN

I am after illness
as a valley
after a monsoon,
damp and disfigured.

I am bedridden,
an old woman
or less.
Driftwood with roots
torn and my history
of slow dusk hills erased.

I am a beached thing
and winter a fortress
gray and enormous.

There are precedents
in these matters.

Faith withers,
the sea-gates break.
Even strong swimmers drown
or wake as a shell intact
on a blanched shore,

raw fibers in the morphology
of sin,
purpose obscure.

The definitions of loss
are inadequate.

Somewhere a startled
sea beast retraces
its route and finds
boundaries decayed,
cliffs indifferent

and the path back
frozen and lost,
gone.

I inch into the subterfuge
of dawn, my selves separate
and crawl into the fenced world,

an amnesiac reconstructing
by instinct the need
to pray and sing.

A DOG'S YAWN

Come to me, dusk,
as if you were the first
and last of your kind,
a clay-painted savage
of the forest,
shy as a deer
and certain as a mountain
that has always been
anchoring the horizon.

I cannot harm you.
Peer not from your blind
of firs and pine but boldly
enter and take as master
this woman, this easy prey.
I have been idle since morning,
my life, like this day,
a dog's yawn.

Now afternoon withers.
The dog on the porch stirs.
And this is not a confession.

I am not the first felled
by seasons immune to negotiation
and the horror that what is,
is and has always and will.
It is the obvious
we battle,
the retractable surfaces
of day and the cycles
of gravity and burial.

We learn slow as the hospital
chart of a terrible fever.
We learn like cripples
at a waltz.
Our legacy is a beggar's dawn

where stripped and thin
we begin again,
as always, from scratch.

I learn from the dog.
Day was hot.
Night will be cooler.

GARDEN POEM

This spring I am luminous
with female promise.
I am dirt-dark, inscrutable
and fertile.

I bend in my warm garden
bare feet muddy.
No one would doubt my purpose,
my intrinsic connections
to ground and womb.
My urgency.

I am permitted secrets again,
as if I were pregnant,
sacred, what waits
for the ember.

From seeds I make squash
and beefsteak tomatoes grow.
Their slow lime points
rise from the earth
and I know loss
is an illusion,

is the tossed shell
in which the sea
is infinitely repeated,
refined, embossed by the surgery
of waves.

It survives implacable.
You cannot know it.

I stand on my hot hillside
of prickly pear and agave,
longing for the patience
of cactus,
willing to wait a century
before I scratch the sky.

Below, beneath hedges, orange
bird of paradise glints.
A sense of white roses,
their fragrance, unique, persists.
The sky is a blue wash,
a kind of smiling mouth.

I could laugh once and crack
the walls of the world.

LULLABY FOR SINNERS

Sleep now.
Slip down in darkness sweet
and dreamless as the dreams
of cows.
Let night take you
as one of her own.
You are warm earth tones,
mahogany, brown wool, the skin
of cellos and atonement.
Your name is plateau crow,
mouth a gash of obsidian.
Your wounds are illusions,
without substance.
Ambivalence is circular
and casts no shadow.
It cannot harm you.
After ash and anger,
sealed graves and afternoons
of suspended blooms
and visions
multiple and inexact,
descent ends as it began
in a starswirl of perpetual
innocent birth.
Let primitive reference points
return to you like the swallows.
Up and down.
Day and night.
Sleep and that frenzied other.
Sleep.
This is the song
your mother longed to sing,
but forgot.
You are her only child,
born when night opened
and clouds collided
in passion with rock.

You are her cherished one,
the ember that glows
in the fog shroud
ambulance red
as the eye of your origin.
Fear nothing.

POEM FOR THE OBSESSED

For you who must nest
at the thorn's edge,

eyes flecked and hard
as opals and sleepless,
certain of your destiny,

release will come worm
slow in random inches.

This is the lesson of history.

The betrayal of the self
consumes and guts
as surely as the blood
of wars.

You say lamplight scars
the sockets where you
once had eyes.

The air, stale with longing
chokes your chest.
It is unspeakable.

Then consider the elegance
and serenity of rock
and be mute.

Your inventions and songs
are obsolete and your struggle
the spasms of a lunatic.

They who love you contingently
will never anoint with olive
oil or bend once to wash
your blistered feet.

The grail you bring is dented,
inadequate and the gold
of legend centuries gone.
Make do without it.

Depart before you wake
ancient and marooned
in a ward for amnesiacs
and fools from a bankrupt court.

Inform the survivors.
The roads are impassable
and hills empty
of all but rock.

Your youth is lost
and the limp permanent.
You cannot get even.

THERE WILL COME A SUNSET

There will come a sunset
pastel and protracted
above red-splashed leaves.

You will see the intricacy
of trees bending.
Their mute architecture
will astound you.

Birds will suspend journeys
and perch on your balcony
considering your strange shape,
your mode of hunting,
and forgive.

Dark hills will fall
harpooned by the tongues
of shadows. The sky pinkens,
sweetens and the sun melts
pale orange, mirrory,
clearly alive.

You will hear cars swishing
and clapping, barking,
the motor of a low-slung plane
and children calling one another
with urgency,

as if night were final
and they, lovers parted
forever.

You will have a rare clarity
and sense of abundance.
The spectacle of darkness
stalking in waves and shades
of blue will both arouse
and calm you.

You will wonder if you are saved.
You are not.
But something enormous rises
like a redwood thrusting
skyward from underbrush.

A shadow is cast and lingers.

JACARANDA

Leaning naked into cricket air
in a June afternoon
of jacaranda falling
I am fourteen again,
a suntanned insomniac,
a beacon, hot blood pumping neon.

The woman unfolding.
I was still girl of the corsage
and duskfall.
Still girl of the pastel frocks,
ivory cameo and parasol.

My voice was a rushing of bells.
My fingers could charm snakes
and renegade moons.
I bent into sun-draped waterfalls
and was whispered to, caressed.

My girl mouth floated smiles.
I called myself amethyst,
opal, pearl.
My decisions were enormous—
to pick white roses
or braid silk ribbons in my hair.

I was a leaf-eater with tapered
giraffe neck and eyes like fists
damp with a promise of abundance,
vineyards, peach orchards,
a valley of walnut trees.

From my window the sky
was the color of flamingos.
And dusk fell soft as a flute
or a late June breeze rustling
jacaranda.

SAPPHIRE BAY

Sailing from St. John island
to Sapphire Bay
the wind suddenly broke.

The sea sucked in her breath
and demure with fraud
closed her green embroidered eyes.

No one spoke.
And we bobbed as buoys bob
becalmed at the edge of the world.

Depth was the only dimension.
I knew the heart was liquid
and never slept.

I did not fear the storm
or glassy acres
where I might drown,

my last breaths engraved
and repeated in the funhouse
mirrors of the sea.

It was the sense of an other
that startled,
an inexplicable juncture

absolute and undeniable
as a virulent form of madness
when the brain dampens

the ordinary masks dissolve
and we know our lives
as frail corridors

illusionary channels
in a sea feeding unrelenting
in a process alien

as a lost art
on an undiscovered star.

TRANSFORMATIONS IN GREEN

There are entire continents
beyond my folly.
Warm pirate zones
of subtle sea-femininities
and banyan hills
of mangos and emeralds.

Night has lilac teeth
and whispers of white
Madagascar jasmine.

Here the secrets of hurricanes
are given,
their swirling circular lust
to mate,
to crease the sky with their own
and spawn in what would be barren.

The moon erupts pearl-tongued
and forgiving.

I am a leaf-eater embroidered
by sudden green rain.
I am the pattern on the tortoise
shell where the sea etched
her dazzling green history.

In a just-born ridge
above painted coves
and green hypnotized cliffs
I bury fury, wild eyes
and the evil that glows.

I will gather green judgment
from ferns and flamed shadows.

Beyond certainties of death
and obvious ruin
there is a further wilderness,
awesome, named for a luminous
warrior king.

Here, in rum-sweet air,
original green palm hill
I will with jade breath enter
into delicate green covenants

and know my life as a psalm.

WEST INDIES PRAYER

Wakening from graceless
hibernated half sleep
into the spangle-lit
more than trance
of Barbados,

floral/coral.

My dead tongue says
cassia, orange orchids
and open coconuts,
open archaic brown thunder
in raw banyan hills.

Take back the bad
black bells of hell
and open hot rain,
make me whole/clean,
with eyes enough
and limbs enough
for one last
not haunted
not frantic
not broken
song.

Open.

Absolve.

I have been lone
scavenger of the harbor.
Our Lady of Blood
and moon-induced frenzies
shouting outrage into clouds
shallow and aghast,
my mouth bruised
by curses and dirge.

Forgive.
Let this be the letting,
the jettisoning from safe
self-debased and implacable pain
into an other,
a transformation,
a shedding
and release.

In the port at St. George,
wharf laden with baskets
of ginger and nutmeg,

the concurrent pieces
of my life float
the ocean
and are gone.

The cream-green seaskin
    splits,
the hatchery empties
and it is terrible
to mourn in summer

when rivers glint lost
beneath mangos and almost-
glimpsed French church steeples
rising on flamboya hills
the color of fire
and resonating with the cries
of chickens.

Here I cannot hide alpine
in my private crystal-hearted
    winter,
my diamond-bitch winter
where I have masqueraded
as sister of night owls
and albino hawks.

On Grand Anse Beach
I am encircled by women
in cobalt and crimson
print gingham, waving
hand-sewn dresses
like flags across
the warm sands.

The world dissolves
behind blue stripes
and red dots shimmering
like a flock of preening
plumed and sun-struck
jungle birds.

I am sanctified/opulent
and would dare.

In Grenada, the boulevard
is vine-swallowed.
Women pass,
boxes of cola bottles
balanced on their heads,

and one can resist
by sheer grace.

There is always the void,
the dark/slow/amber/glowing
and becalmed gulfs of what is intractable.
So what?

In the shantytown,
windowless shacks
and broken boards,
women sew, beige and brown
piglets at their feet,

in the shadow of a dynasty
of green volcanos.

I flow as their river
flows, following a track
of old tires, rusty buckets,
fallen pears, oranges,
breadfruits and mangos,

reaching for the warm center,
the final green corridor,
where two wizened women
lean against a water pump
discussing death,
the scriptures
and the incorruptibility of the flesh.

NO MORE THE ANIMAL LIFE

Thou hast drunk blood
from thine own lies
and drained thy hell creatures

dry.

Insubstantial and silent,
the raving horde unrising.
Still in dark hacked obsolescence
the picked clean carcass floats.

Tell us of your personal
muse.
Do.

How you burned the candle
down the center
and your fingers turned smooth
as new May moons.
You sent the little boys away
and bricked your doors,

warmed by a purpose not ordinary.

Remember?

And the barrio in July.
Heat fierce and searing.
How it suddenly quieted,

as if the young men fixing
cars and grandmothers
visiting from Tijuana had all
been summoned to one shared

siesta.

Branden Street sat becalmed,
sun numbed and deserted
in a 2 p. m. of the invisible

fence.

(It didn't apply to you.)

Or tell us about Janis
with a needle in her arm,
swallowing the final blue ember,

her veins a sea.

Don't be shy.

You were quite the lurid one.
Such a daring girl.
You consorted with demons
and vanquished them.
There, dear.
We'll mail you the grail.

Enter now the brutal clouds
of winter strung low
above reticent trees
stripped as if by machete.

It's your new home, pal.
Like it?

This is where the heart sleeps,
with its archaic fever
and sheered wings,

and sleeps, too, your despoiled
song, your wounded, abandoned one.

No wicked monograms
or hills of rare and splendid
starving lynx.
No rose petals perched in bowls,
red as blood in noon sun.

No more the animal life.

NAVIGATING BY BELLS

It was a Sunday after rain.
I could navigate by bells.

The December clouds floated slow
as if they too drank vodka
and slept late.
The air was lace.

I held my long black hair
with ivory combs.
I wore perfume from Mozambique
and a strand of amber pearls.

Your eyes were blue, brilliant
as sunstruck glacial ice,
irresistible as the metallic
flames of prized ores.

You sat wrapped in a silk-
lined quilt and read
Pound out loud
and whispered,
your hair looks like wood,
and the ground cracked.

Noon was blue stars,
blue asters, the Indian Ocean,
more blue than I asked for.

The hills were immaculate
as rows of just-washed
terra cotta pots.

Trees stood engraved
unnaturally green,
pagan, silent, hot.

I thought, it could end now.
Close like a Chinese paper fan
flapping shut.